THE

Old Man
LIVING IN MY HEAD

*One Guy's Musings
About the Bible*

DON EVERTS

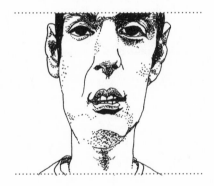

IVP Books

An imprint of InterVarsity Press
Downers Grove, Illinois

InterVarsity Press
P.O. Box 1400, Downers Grove, IL 60515-1426
World Wide Web: www.ivpress.com
E-mail: email@ivpress.com

InterVarsity Press® is the book-publishing division of InterVarsity Christian
Fellowship/USA®, a student movement active on campus at hundreds of
universities, colleges and schools of nursing in the United States of America,
and a member movement of the International Fellowship of Evangelical
Students. For information about local and regional activities, write Public
Relations Dept., InterVarsity Christian Fellowship/USA, 6400 Schroeder Rd.,
P.O. Box 7895, Madison, WI 53707-7895, or visit the IVCF website at
<www.intervarsity.org>.

All Scripture quotations, unless otherwise indicated, are taken from the Holy
Bible, Today's New International Version™ Copyright © 2001 by
International Bible Society. All rights reserved.

Illustrations and design by Matt Smith

ISBN 978-0-8308-3612-3

Printed in the United States of America ∞

Library of Congress Cataloging-in-Publication Data

Everts, Don, 1971-
    The old man living in my head: one guy's musings about the Bible/
Don Everts.
        p. cm.—(One guy's head)
    Includes bibliographical references.
    ISBN-13: 978-0-8308-3612-3 (pbk.: alk. paper)
    1. Apologetics-Miscellanea. 2. Bible—Evidences, authority,
    etc.—Miscellanea.I. Title.
    BT1103.E942007
    220.1—dc22

                                                            2007031478

P	15	14	13	12	11	10	9	8	7	6	5	4	3	2	1
Y	19	18	17	16	15	14	13	12	11	10	09	08	07		

Contents

INTRODUCTION:
MY HEAD

Welcome to my head.

In the following pages I plan to introduce you to some of the various ideas that live up in my head. And you'll have the pleasure of meeting one strange idea up there in particular. That idea tends to act like an old man—frail and bent over and slow moving and *quite stubborn*. He wears an old-fashioned suit and is always clutching a big black book with both of his frail arms. THE OLD MAN CLUTCHING THE BIG BLACK BIBLE is his name, but the rest of the ideas up there just call him THE OLD MAN.

But I'm getting ahead of myself. Before you meet this one, I think it's important to let you know why anyone should care about my head at all.

For the full answer, you'd really have to go on the full tour of my head.[1] But for now let me just say that my goal for trying to honestly describe what goes on up in my head (a potentially embarrassing endeavor) is not to provide some sort of intellectual peep show. It's really not. My first goal is to honestly describe what I believe about the Bible—and how I go about believing it. My second goal is to encourage more honest self-reflection and more relaxed conversations among people with heads full of different ideas. My hope is that my own honesty will help us all (myself included) practice the exquisite, everyday, joyful art of thinking more and more all the time.

That's why I'm letting you take a trip into my head to meet THE OLD MAN. But before we get to the formal introductions, I should probably give you a peak into how things generally work up there in my head, so that this introduction of THE OLD MAN makes at least a little sense to you.

Up in my head, ideas walk around like people.

Some folks say that ideas are inert propositional statements and that thinking is like doing science or math: you judge and weigh pieces of data until you find out what's consistent and true. Other folks say that ideas are more like snatches of visceral experience and that thinking is the act of honestly feeling these subjective experiences.

But when I am honest with myself, I have to admit that the ideas up in my head aren't quite so cold and datalike as some say, nor as subjective and experiential as others say. In my head, ideas tend to act more like people: they each have their own personality, their own style, their own way of getting along in my head. And each of them has a story to tell me.

For example, this old man that lives in my head is an idea with a story to tell about the Bible. It's not like he's a dispassionate propositional statement about the Bible waiting to be examined or some existentially honest experience with the Bible waiting to be felt. It's like that idea is really up there. It has a personality and acts like . . . well, in this case, like an old man. An old man with a story to tell.

THE OLD MAN isn't alone, of course. There are all kinds of ideas living up there, in this house of living ideas. And each one has its own story. Some have been up there since I was a kid (such as THE GOLD OF BOOKS, who tells a story about how great it is to be a reader); others are new ideas that walked into my head recently when I was reading a new book (for example, SHINY HAPPY GLOBALIZATION, who tells a story about the upside of our increasingly global economies and technologies).

That's what ideas are like up in my head. Thinking, then, is when I call a house meeting and all of the ideas (well, most of them) come to the living room in my head. The living room is where the ideas hang out together, tell their stories to each other, ask questions, argue, fight, agree and so on. Stuff you would do if you lived in a house with a bunch of other people and hung out together in the living room. When the ideas are interacting with each other in the living room—I'm thinking.

Sounds a bit chaotic, I guess. But if you've ever lived in a crowded house with a bunch of other people, you know very well that every house wants order. This order doesn't have to be explicit *(George is in charge!)*, but it is definite *(George is a fifth-year senior?! I guess he gets the big bedroom, huh?)*.

As in any real house, the house of living ideas in my head has social hierarchies (some ideas have been around longer and hold more sway), tensions (some new ideas that walk into my head aren't liked by anyone and are eventually kicked right out of my head) and complexities (not all the stories jibe perfectly, which means the ideas have some talking to do if they plan to live in the same head together). This is why getting the ideas to interact in the living room (thinking) is so crucial (and, usually, quite interesting).

Anyway, up in my head there is this one idea called, simply, THE OLD MAN. He sits on a stool in the living room of my head and has quite a story to tell in that feeble old voice of his. And all the while he's clutching that huge black Bible on his lap like his life depended on it.

But how did he get up there in the first place? And what, exactly, is his story? And what does he have to say for himself when other ideas start peppering him with questions? And, in the end, am I really going to let this old idea stay living up there in my head?

Well, those questions are what this book is all about. Which means it's time to get on with the introductions. If you turn the page, you can enter my house of living ideas and meet this infamous idea for yourself.

Chapter 1

MEET THE OLD MAN

There is an old man living inside my head.

And he's clutching a big black Bible.

He's a very old man. Tired, old, wrinkled face. Terribly wrinkled. He's painfully bent over with age. Thinning arms and neck and hair. His ears and nose have gotten a bit big for his face. Very pale skin, though very little skin is actually showing, come to think of it. Just his thin, vein-covered hands, his wrinkled face, those big ears and that thin neck poking out of the starched white collar of that dress shirt he always wears.

Speaking of that white shirt and that old suit of his, he's quite old-fashioned, wearing nothing that's been in style for quite some time. To be honest, his clothes look really uncomfortable to me— too tucked in and straight and all.

What you need to know about this old guy is that, though he may look frail, he's got some fire in him. He's a stubborn old man. A patient, strong sort of stubborn. Some would say ignorant.

He clutches a Bible tightly with his two skinny arms. He's a short man, and the Bible he's clutching is large, so it takes his whole arms to hold that one old book on his thin little lap. But that's OK; he wants no other books. He's satisfied with that one. He'll read other books, but he never holds them like he does this one. In fact, he always seems to have this big old Bible open on his lap as a sort of desk to hold any other books as he skims through them.

He really likes his big black book. When his thin fingers turn the ancient, yellowing pages, they do so really slowly, with a kind of patience or kindness. The pages make a soft sound, sort of like leaves in the fall, but softer and more muted than that.

I'm not sure when he first moved into my brain. I do know I've kicked him out a few times—he is just so old-fashioned. And the new guys and gals who roam in and out of my brain always make fun of him.

Some ideas say he's an idiot and walk away laughing and shaking their heads without ever talking to him. Some other ideas are carrying that same big black book, but they aren't clutching it so desperately as he is. They usually can't, since they are carrying around other books as well—some they've written themselves, others they've been sold. And these other ideas sound much more impressive and clever and fresh to me. THE OLD MAN always seems to say the same thing.

These new ideas mock him so derisively, so intelligently, so cleverly. And I have been swayed a few times. Kicked him right out.

But other times I sit and listen to his story over and over. And something in it rings true to me. I've seen him go the rounds with all the new ideas that visit my brain. I see them make fun of him and I hear their sharp questions. But when they stick around long enough to really talk with him, I like his answers. His clothes still strike me as stiff and uncomfortable, but his story is incredible.

Well, you just need to meet the old guy. You'll see what I mean. He looks a little silly. And he mostly reads from that book rather than just talking, which is hard to get used to. But I think you'll see why he's grown on me over time.

Chapter 2

THE OLD MAN'S STORY

Most ideas who stroll into my head ask THE OLD MAN questions as soon as they see him. Not too polite. But they usually seem shocked that he's in there, so they fire away. He rarely responds to their impatient jabs.

But if they seem really interested, he'll start to tell his story. And if they cut in with questions, he insists, "No interrupting. No questions until you've heard the whole story. Then I'll answer whatever questions you like." He's pretty polite and gentlemanly, and his voice is both shaky and resolute, if that's possible. Shaky with age. Resolute with something that comes from within him. A crackly, almost raspy old voice coming from a set of fatigued lungs and vocal chords that have done their time. His story goes something like this:

"First, I want to let you know that there are three scenes in my story. I hope all of you young'uns like stories with three scenes in them. A little like a stage play or motion picture, I guess!"

THE OLD MAN pauses as if waiting for laughter or applause or something. He clears his throat, his hands holding tightly to the book in his lap.

"Scene One: God. Once upon a time there was a God. And he was invisible.

"Now, he happened to be the only true God. (All other supposed gods, it turns out, were silly made-up lies.) He had created everything that was—out of nothing. Before him there was nothing at all. Except himself, of course. And then he created a whole universe and nestled in the middle of it a little world full of people. There were also animals and trees and wind and such, but God was mostly interested in those people.

"He loved them deeply. And, in spite of his invisibility, he longed to be known by them.

"So he spoke to them in many and various ways—to tell them he loved them, to let them know what he was like, to remind them that all other 'gods' were silly made-up lies. He also wanted to show them why he had made them in the first place and how to get along with joy on that little world he had put them on. So he did. He used soft winds and low clouds, dreams and whispers, bushes and a donkey—just about anything he could get his hands on that would help him speak clearly into their little ears."

At this point, THE OLD MAN pauses and smiles at the other ideas sitting around him in the living room up in my head. He catches his shallow breath and then speaks again.

"Scene Two: Jesus. But it turns out he was saving up a real doozy! And it wasn't a surprise, either. He told the little people about it time and time again. 'One day you're gonna hear from me like you've never imagined. One day . . .' And then that day came.

"God's real doozy was that he got born as a little person right on their little world. He was named Jesus, and what a doozy he was! He was still that invisible God who had created everything and so loved those people, and he really was a little person who could look them right in the eyes. Nearly unbelievable! It *was* like nothing they had ever seen before. This fleshly Jesus was God revealing himself in perfect clarity. Speaking right into people's ears. No other way God had ever revealed himself (burning up a bush, speaking in a voice from a cloud) compared to having God himself right there, walking around with the people.

"And everything that Jesus did was an announcement to the people. His life and death (he lived only a short time) were like the perfect, divine Sentence. Or Word. Ultimate clarity on what God was like, how much he loved the little people, how to get along in joy on that little world. Jesus' personality, teachings, posture, actions, suffering, resurrection were the ultimate, end-all Sentence from God.

"This doozy, Jesus, was himself the ultimate point of clarity that God had always been building up to. Not one part of Jesus—the whole shebang. It wasn't just his teachings, it was also the way he treated people. It wasn't just the posture of his whole life; it was also the posture of his death—and his return from the dead. (Which is a story unto itself—one I'd love to share sometime. The best story ever, actually.) But anyway, what I'm saying is that you couldn't just take one part of Jesus and leave the rest. Jesus was Jesus. *The* Sentence. The invisible God's ultimate moment of clear, beautiful speech.

"And then he left. Jesus, that is. Not the way anyone figured Scene Two would end at all!

" 'Why do you have to leave?' Jesus' student-followers asked him, desperation in their voices.

" 'Trust me,' he said. 'It'll be even better. Scene Three is great!'

"All of the little people who were his student-followers wanted to know what could be so great about Scene Three.

" 'Do you see my legs?' he asked them.

"They nodded their little heads.

" 'These legs are little—like yours, right? So you can see right into my eyes.'

"They all smiled. They couldn't help it. His eyes were so beautiful and so near.

" 'But I can only walk so far with these little legs and tiny lungs. But I love *everyone*. I love you; I love those people over there; I love this guy that's all the way on the other side of this little world.'

"Jesus' student-followers nodded. They knew how wonderful it was to meet him themselves. They remembered clearly what it was like to hear the Sentence for the first time.

" 'And guess what?'

"Their eyes all opened wide at the excited tone in Jesus' voice. 'What?' they asked together.

"Jesus smiled. *'You* are in Scene Three.'

" 'Us?' they asked.

"Jesus nodded thoughtfully and looked each of them in the eyes. And he told them all about it. And Scene Three turned out to be just as he had said."

Here THE OLD MAN leans forward, his eyes wide. Despite themselves, some of the other ideas up in my head seem a bit caught up in his story. Others look deathly bored.

"Scene Three: The Church. After Jesus left, the student-followers knew what they were to do. They were to testify about Jesus. To sing out the Sentence exactly as they had heard it. Jesus had told them it was their job, because they had been with him from the beginning. They had seen more of his posture and teachings and words and sufferings and miraculous return from the dead than anyone else. So they were the perfect ones to be witnesses of the Sentence. To repeat it over and over again. There *was* no other sentence, after all. Nothing else that could ever be said could compare with the life of Jesus lived up close, God whispering into their ears with crystal clarity. It was God's absolute best. His ultimate cry.

"So the student-followers were the church. The Keepers of the Sentence.

"And how had Jesus told them to keep it? By repeating it over and over again to other little people who hadn't ever heard the Sentence. People who had no idea what God was really like and how much he loved them and why he had put them on that little world. And when these little people would ask to be student-followers of Jesus, they too would be the church. And they too would go around echoing the Sentence to anyone who would listen.

"But not yet. Like I said, the student-followers knew exactly what they were supposed to do. But they waited. Because Jesus had told them to. 'Wait until God sends a wind ripping around you and into your very hearts. God will be in that wind. And through that wind we will be with you so close—we will be *inside* you.' Their eyes had gotten big when Jesus told them that part. Scene Three, they were finding out, *was* starting to sound like quite a scene!

" 'And this Wind of God,' Jesus went on, 'will remind you of everything I have said and done. It will testify about me, just as you will be testifying. This Wind will echo the Sentence wherever you go. Without it, Scene Three would be impossible for you.'

"And so they waited. God *did* send the Wind, and it *did* rip around them and go into their very hearts. And it *did* remind them of the Sentence. And with the Wind blowing all around them, and within their hearts, the little people spoke the Sentence over and over again.

"Wherever the Sentence is heard and accepted, the Wind rips around people and goes into their hearts. The Sentence becomes a part of them. And they find out more every day about how much God loves them and what God is like and why he created them and put them on this little world.

"They keep speaking the Sentence just as they heard it, living forever after as Keepers of the Sentence."

THE OLD MAN in my brain loves telling his story. His eyes close at times in the telling and the story comes out almost in a hum. When he's done, he pauses a moment for effect (he really loves that story) and then accepts questions from any ideas who've bothered to stick around for the whole story.

Chapter 3

THE WRITERS
OF THE BIBLE

Some of the ideas up in my head are quite unsatisfied with the story and have plenty of questions (and comments!) for THE OLD MAN. I've heard several Q&A times. Many different ideas pepper THE OLD MAN with questions. YOUTHFUL CYNICISM THAT QUESTIONS ALL AUTHORITY is always one of the more vocal ideas after THE OLD MAN tells his story. But plenty of others chime in as well. After thinking about the authority of Scripture (THE OLD MAN telling his story) something like this tends to go on up in my head.

YOUTHFUL CYNICISM's face is flat. Unimpressed. His long, black bangs mostly cover his eyes and any expression his face might contain. He starts in with a voice that is laced with sarcasm. "Nice story, old-timer. But what does that story have to do with that book you're clutching?"

"This book"—he looks down at the book

clutched in his arms and smiles—"is the Sentence. Written down."

"But it's a whole book. There are lots of sentences in it." YOUTHFUL CYNICISM looks pleased with himself. "Which one are you talking about?"

"I'm talking about *the* Sentence—the life and death of God as a little person. The Story of Jesus. All his words, his teachings, his treatment of people, his answers to questions, his terrible suffering, his death, his resurrection, his words about Scene Three. All of it! He was God's Word." THE OLD MAN looks down at the book in his arms as his frail voice recovers. "This is that Word written down."

"You mean the Bible? But how can you trust that book at all?" YOUTHFUL CYNICISM looks incredulous. "It was written by these 'little people,' as you call them, who had their own agendas and pet opinions and biases."

THE OLD MAN looks up from the Bible and nods strongly as if in thought. "Yes, they did have an agenda."

YOUTHFUL CYNICISM is more animated than usual at this point, his young voice growing a bit high. "See? So, how can you trust what they wrote down? Do you really believe that Bible right there in your skinny arms contains anything that remotely resembles the life Jesus lived two thousand years ago on the other side of the world?"

THE OLD MAN living in my head looks down at

the Bible before responding in his ancient, level voice. "Oh yes."

"You're kidding! You yourself said the men who supposedly wrote the different parts of that Bible had their own agendas and that—"

THE OLD MAN leans forward a bit on his wooden stool, still clutching the big black Bible, and interrupts. "I said they had *an* agenda. An agenda that was given to them." YOUTHFUL CYNICISM doesn't like being interrupted like that, right when he's building up a head of steam. But THE OLD MAN continues. "Would you like to know about that agenda?"

"Sure." YOUTHFUL CYNICISM THAT QUESTIONS ALL AUTHORITY (that's his full name) always seems to have shorter answers when he doesn't know where the conversation is going.

"It was a great agenda." THE OLD MAN slowly opens the big black book in his hands and flips a few pages and then begins to speak, his voice carrying a reverent tone. "As Jesus himself told his followers, 'When the Advocate comes, whom I will send to you from the Father—the Spirit of truth who goes out from the Father—he will testify about me. And you also must testify, for you have been with me from the beginning.' "[1]

YOUTHFUL CYNICISM, CIRCULAR REASONING IS INFERIOR REASONING and many other ideas stand up, looking surprised, almost offended as the old guy reads from the big black Bible. YOUTH-FUL CYNICISM speaks up. "Hey, you can't do that!"

"I can't do what?" THE OLD MAN looks up in surprise.

"You can't quote from the book that's in question! Isn't that like defining a word by using the same word in the definition? That's illegal!"

THE OLD MAN looks confused. "Son, can you think of a better place to look to find out the agenda of the people who wrote down this book?" There's a pause at this point, so THE OLD MAN takes up talking again, his voice slow, careful. "The church was relentlessly repeating a message. Is it so hard to fathom that their reason for repeating the message might be found by looking at that message? They had heard the Sentence. And the Sentence himself had told them to go and repeat the story of his life and death and resurrection everywhere. So that's what they did, including the parts where he had told them, 'You are witnesses of these things' and 'Go and make disciples of all nations, . . . teaching them to obey everything I have commanded you.' "[2]

YOUTHFUL CYNICISM raises his arms in protest. "You did it again! Twice!"

"And I'll do it more, if you want. Listen, son, you seemed to imply earlier that the people who wrote this book here had an agenda that colored their writing. And that this agenda made them want to write down something different about Jesus than what really happened, making their written words suspect from a historical perspective. Did I read your implication correctly?" THE OLD MAN looks evenly at YOUTHFUL CYNICISM, who's standing in front of him.

"Absolutely."

"And *what was* this agenda of theirs?"

But before YOUTHFUL CYNICISM can answer, another idea stands up and begins speaking. Her name is POWER ALWAYS CORRUPTS. "Well, probably to create followers for *themselves!* They were humans, after all—selfish beasts like all other humans. They created these miracle stories after the fact so that more people would want to follow this new religion they'd founded. Paul and those guys made it all up to get gazillions of followers!"

THE OLD MAN looks genuinely confused. "Well, I find that agenda . . . hard to believe. For many reasons. But what so convinces *you*, ma'am, that these men who lived two thousand years ago had that specific motivation, which would then cause them to write down supposedly fabricated stories about the life of Jesus?"

POWER ALWAYS CORRUPTS smiles a crooked smile. "Do you have any idea how much money these guys were making?"

"You mean before they were killed for repeating these stories about Jesus?"

POWER ALWAYS CORRUPTS continues, "Yeah. People were forking over all their dough to the church, and these guys had to love all that power and money."

THE OLD MAN living in my head looks closely at the hands of POWER ALWAYS CORRUPTS at this point, with an odd look on his face. "And how do you know that was happening back then? Did you read that somewhere?"

POWER ALWAYS CORRUPTS looks confused. "Well, doesn't it say in . . . OK, I get your point." She puts her hands on her hips before the bent old man. "Listen, there are lots of other manuscripts from the time other than the Bible, you know. Wasn't Josephus a historian of the time? And didn't he write about all of this?"

THE OLD MAN nods his head. "Sure. And everything he wrote corroborates the history contained in this book in my arms. But do you think *he* had an agenda too? Josephus, that is."

YOUTHFUL CYNICISM pipes up before POWER ALWAYS CORRUPTS can answer. "Listen, I don't know anything about Josephus. But I do know that a historian is more trustworthy than a bunch of religious people starting their own religion. They weren't impartially writing down facts; they had their own take on everything, their own agenda. You yourself said they had an agenda."

THE OLD MAN nods strongly again, some of his

wispy gray hairs sticking up. "Yes. A strong one! So strong that it directed their teaching and writing every step of the way. And their agenda was to pass on what they had received without altering it. That overwhelming agenda is everywhere throughout this book." THE OLD MAN looks down at the big book in his hands. "Would you like some examples?"

YOUTHFUL CYNICISM sighs audibly and shrugs, drooping back down into his couch. "Sure, old-timer."

"Well, one of the Gospel writers introduced his writing this way." THE OLD MAN opens the large book again and slowly flips a few large, incredibly thin pages before reading, "Many have undertaken to draw up an account of the things that have been fulfilled among us, just as they were handed down to us by those who from the first were eyewitnesses and servants of the word. . . . Since I myself have carefully investigated everything from the beginning, I too decided to write an orderly account . . . so that you may know the certainty of the things you have been taught."[3]

SOURCE CRITICISM, an educated-sounding member of the Higher Criticism Gang who always has a story to tell about where the books of the Bible "really" came from, pipes up from the back of the living room, an unmistakable sound of superiority in his voice. "So *many* people were writing down this life of Jesus? What if they weren't all as careful as this Luke fellow?"

THE OLD MAN nods and continues in his strained old voice, "Well, John was another Gospel writer who wrote some epistles as well. Here's how he talked about his task as a writer: 'That which was from the beginning, which we have heard, which we have seen with our eyes, which we have looked at and our hands have touched—this we proclaim concerning the Word of life. . . . We proclaim to you what we have seen and heard, so that you also may have fellowship with us.' "[4]

SOURCE CRITICISM's head falls into his hands and he shakes his head slowly.[5]

"He *touched* Jesus?" POWER ALWAYS CORRUPTS looks confused at this point.

"Yes," THE OLD MAN says. "That first-person contact was important to the early church. It was essential that those who had seen Jesus and had been with him from the beginning got to broadcast what they saw and heard and, yes, touched. Repeating that message far and wide became their top priority."

POWER ALWAYS CORRUPTS nods condescendingly. "And that was their agenda, you say?"

"That agenda wasn't just an *agenda*; it was their new life." THE OLD MAN smiles, looking a bit silly as all the ideas in my head see that he's lost a couple teeth. But he doesn't seem to notice and goes right on. "Hearing the Sentence had changed them forever and they wanted to share that. That one writer, John, said that writing the story down actually gave him joy!" THE OLD MAN coughs a bit at this point, his frail throat needing to recover.

REDACTION CRITICISM (another member of the Higher Criticism Gang) pipes up from the back of the room in a British accent. "OK. But what about Paul? He came on the scene much later. And he *supposedly* wrote practically all of the New Testament."

THE OLD MAN nods. "Paul did write many of the letters in the New Testament. *After* he heard the message himself, *after* he had the Wind from God rip around him and go into his heart and *after* he was taken into the church and taught. And guess what the Wind (which Jesus sent to testify about himself) and the church (the Keepers of the Sentence) taught Paul, our new guy on the scene?"

REDACTION CRITICISM looks unamused. "OK, what?"

THE OLD MAN smiles and his eyes almost close as he speaks, "To proclaim Jesus. That's it."

REDACTION CRITICISM still looks unamused. "That's it?"

"Yes! And this overwhelming call to proclaim Jesus is clear in the writings *about* Paul—you can look at Acts if you like—and is everywhere in Paul's writings as well. For example, Paul wrote to one church, 'I resolved to know nothing while I was with you except Jesus Christ and him crucified.' And he also wrote, 'What I received, I passed on to you.' "[6]

THE OLD MAN flips some more pages and continues on in his patient, thin voice. "And when Paul was raising up younger people to carry on this work of being Keepers of the Sentence, he told them, 'Guard the good deposit that was entrusted to you.' "[7] THE OLD MAN sometimes goes off for quite a while, just reading from that book of his as if he has all the time in the world.[8] He'll read from letters Paul wrote to young leaders and say things like "This is what the church was about. They were Keepers of the Sentence! You know what Paul said the church should insist on in their leaders?"[9]

And on and on. Many ideas living in my head exchange knowing looks as THE OLD MAN's fingers work the thin pages with care.

Somewhere along the line YOUTHFUL CYNICISM, still standing in the middle of the living room in my head, brushes his long bangs out of his eyes. "So, you're saying all the dudes who wrote that book you're holding thought they had received the truth and were passing on the truth as they wrote?"

"All of them." THE OLD MAN smiles and starts slowly turning the large, faded pages and starts to read again. "The writer of the letter to the Hebrews writes, 'We must pay the most careful attention, therefore, to what we have heard, so that we do not drift away. . . . This salvation, which was first announced by the Lord, was confirmed to us by those who heard him.' "[10] More painfully slow page turning and more rolled eyes from other ideas.[11]

Eventually THE OLD MAN notices the coughing and blank stares. He smiles politely, looking around at the ideas around him. "This is *everywhere* in the New Testament. You can't read the thing without getting the very clear sense that the church had a culture dominated by telling this story. And being careful to tell it just as they had heard it. They were the Keepers of the Sentence after all."

YOUTHFUL CYNICISM shrugs. "But that doesn't prove they were right, does it?"

THE OLD MAN slowly taps the big book on his lap. "It proves to me that those who wrote the New Testament were writing under the influence of an agenda. The agenda was strong and pervasive and apparently life-giving to them: to tell the story of Jesus exactly as they had heard it. And that agenda makes me trust their posture as writers."

YOUTHFUL CYNICISM looks as if he's heard a good joke. "But face it—even if they had the *best* of intentions (which I am not as convinced of as you), they were still *human*. There must have been occasions of faulty memory, faulty speech, a misplaced word here or there, a misunderstanding or two or three . . . or four. There's nothing so unbelievable about that."

THE OLD MAN nods. "True enough. A good point. One that I believe God thought of as well.

Which is why he sent the Wind. Jesus himself told his student-followers that the Wind 'will teach you all things and remind you of everything I have said to you.'[12] The Wind was sent to guide the echoing. The Wind came to keep those little human mistakes from getting the whole testimony off track."

CIRCULAR REASONING IS INFERIOR REASONING shakes his head. "I still can't get used to you doing that—quoting from that book to support that book."

POWER ALWAYS CORRUPTS butts in. "And I certainly don't like the idea of God controlling people and *magically* causing them to write."

THE OLD MAN shrugs. "Nothing magical about it. Remember Luke's comments about his own process, his 'careful investigation'? Lots of hard human work, which God was able to keep from straying. If God were overpowering people and literally controlling their pens, we wouldn't have the great literary and linguistic variety that we have among the different writers of the New Testament books. Paul writes like Paul. Mark writes like Mark. John writes totally differently from all of them. God sent his Spirit to 'remind' and to 'teach,' not to dictate. Those were the verbs Jesus used."

"*Supposedly* used," YOUTHFUL CYNICISM says with a smile.

THE OLD MAN smiles back. "According to this book in my arms, yep."

POWER ALWAYS CORRUPTS speaks up from the back of the living room again, not bothering to stand up. "But I'm sure you are aware that there were many other books—gospels and epistles and histories—that were also written. But these other books were voted out by some patriarchal, biased group of old men. They decided what got in and what stayed out, just by a vote."

What a buzz this creates! Many ideas in my head perk up at this point and the heat in the room gets dialed up. It's quite an interesting exchange that ensues.

But, to be honest, some of the ideas living in my head don't stay to listen to THE OLD MAN's response. SOURCE CRITICISM and his buddies (the whole Higher Criticism Gang of relatively young ideas) walk away at this point. Some of them leave my brain entirely. They leave with superior looks on their faces, shaking their heads and looking back at THE OLD MAN with pity. They usually mutter under their breath as they leave—I can sometimes make out words like "naive," "simpleton" and "batty old man."

But for those who do stay, they'll get to hear what this batty old man has to say about all these different books that didn't get included in that Bible of his and how it was decided what would get in and what wouldn't.

Chapter 4

GETTING THE
STORY WRONG

When POWER ALWAYS CORRUPTS brings up the "other books" that didn't make it into the Bible, the living room in my head really gets hopping—which means a lot of thinking is going on. For example, one really sexy idea,[1] called DA VINCI HAD A NAUGHTY LITTLE SECRET, starts dancing around, and many of the ideas in my head are distracted by this new guy as he throws a comment or two toward THE OLD MAN.

When the living room has settled down enough for the ideas to hear what THE OLD MAN has to say about all this, he launches into an interesting account of how the writings were collected and how this made perfect sense given the nature of Scene Three and all. But before he gets far, YOUTHFUL CYNICISM starts shaking his head, his long bangs swaying back and forth over his dark, incredulous eyes.

"Wait a second!" he says, looking directly into THE OLD MAN's eyes as if challenging him. "But why would people create these other gospels and epistles? Why would anyone 'get the story wrong' if your church culture was so resolutely strong and insistent on always repeating the same story?"

THE OLD MAN smiles slightly, returning YOUTH-FUL CYNICISM's gaze. "Son, you've never read the Sentence, have you?" THE OLD MAN living in my head usually closes his eyes at this point and pauses for a moment or two, as if trying to figure out how to proceed. "This Sentence is a good piece of news that slices deeply into all of the human-produced bad news we've become addicted to as a species. You'd have to read the Sentence for your-self to see, but suffice it to say that there were many people who were too proud, too comfortable, too stiff to receive the Sentence."

The young, slouching figure shrugs his shoul-ders. "So they purposely messed up the story be-cause they didn't like it? Because they wanted to de-rail the church? Because they thought they had a better sentence? I don't get it. What are you suggesting?"

"Well, I don't want to guess as to each of their motives. I am sure it was personal and complex and much more interesting than I could imagine." THE OLD MAN pauses, looking down at the book in his hands for a moment before continuing in his ancient voice. "Well, maybe their motives were . . . boring; I don't know. I do know two things, though. One: The early church had to explicitly guard itself against humans mixing their own human sentences in with the Sentence from God—"

"Wait!" YOUTHFUL CYNICISM leans forward a bit. "What do you mean they had to 'explicitly guard themselves'?"

THE OLD MAN leans forward too. "I mean they knew there would be people who, for whatever reason, would try to import their own human understanding rather than just receiving and passing on the divine Sentence as found in the life of Jesus. They knew that would go on. And you can't miss that if you read this book I'm holding. Might I read a little bit from it?"

POWER ALWAYS CORRUPTS leans back in a couch, folding her arms across her chest. "I can't imagine we could stop you."

THE OLD MAN nods politely at POWER ALWAYS CORRUPTS. "Well, you can read it yourself if you like. It's obvious that the leaders of the church had to remain vigilant against people leading the church astray. Let's see . . ." Here THE OLD MAN opens the book and flips several thin, fragile pages before reading in that feeble but reverent voice of his. "Paul says, 'See to it that no one takes you captive through hollow and deceptive philosophy, which depends on human tradition and the elemental spiritual forces of this world rather than on Christ.'[2] And Peter, who was never one to mince words, wrote, 'In their greed these teachers will exploit you with fabricated stories.' "[3]

At this point (yes, you guessed it!) THE OLD MAN keeps flipping pages and reading in that slow voice of his. I told you early on that it's hard to get used to a guy reading to you all the time. But this old guy is just like that. He clutches that Bible or reads from it. That's about all he does. At least it's what he likes doing the most. Again, I'll spare you the full catalog.[4]

After a while POWER ALWAYS CORRUPTS is staring, obviously bored, up at the ceiling. "Anything else, old man?"

THE OLD MAN smiles. "Believe me, I would love to keep going. But I believe you've seen the point."

YOUTHFUL CYNICISM brushes the bangs out of his eyes. "Which is?"

"Which is that the church recognized that there would be people 'messing the story up,' as you put it. And there were. And that's why they needed to so resolutely echo only what the first student-followers joyfully proclaimed and what the Wind confirmed. That's precisely why the church sought to canonize these books. And that's why the Wind watched over the process—to create a permanent record once and for all that could guide each and every new generation of little people who hear the Sentence.[5]

"Remember, that was God's deep desire. That's the story: God longed for everyone to hear. That was his point in sending Jesus and his point in founding the church and his point in sending his Wind to that church. So that people would hear the clearest, surest, most love-drenched Sentence from the mouth of God ever. The life and death and resurrection of Jesus."

At this point another idea sits up, looking offended. She's a middle-aged idea. And she looks angry. Her name is THE CHURCH IS BANKRUPT (AND HAS HURT ME). She glares over at THE OLD MAN. "Are you preaching at us?!" Sometimes there are incredulous looks from other ideas in my head as well.

THE OLD MAN shakes his head. "Not quite. I am talking about this book in my arms, which all of you asked me about. It's a gift, you see. In this book I encounter the voice of our invisible God. I see him fleshed out intimately, personally, intricately in this person, Jesus. And it's . . . *right in here.* . . ." He begins turning pages again.

YOUTHFUL CYNICISM interrupts. "That's great, old man. I'm very glad for you. Wasn't there a point two somewhere?"

THE OLD MAN stares for a moment and then smiles and nods. "Ah yes. Someone had asked about these other books that didn't get included in the canon of Scripture. I told you that I didn't know why they were written, exactly, but that I did know two things."

THE CHURCH IS BANKRUPT looks over at THE OLD MAN. "The first being that there were all kinds of wackos screwing up the church's message and the church was pissed about that."

The face on THE OLD MAN, wrinkled and pale, looks genuinely confused for a moment. "Um, more or less. . . . The second thing I know is this: God has an enemy."

YOUTHFUL CYNICISM laughs out loud. A thin, sarcastic laugh. "You mean Satan? *The devil?!* Red cape, horns and a pitchfork?"

Wide grins and knowing looks are exchanged among many of the new ideas in my brain at this point. Dozens of ideas, all dressed alike, start jabbing each other in the ribs and pointing at THE OLD MAN and laughing. Each of these ideas have their own names, but they usually roam around together. They are known as the Gang of Invisible Enlightenment Assumptions. Their laughter and jokes fill my mind with their noise.

But not every idea laughs at this point. Some don't necessarily look up or say anything, but I see their heads nodding slightly, their faces grim and sober. TRAGEDY, WAR and THE DIRTY BEGGAR are among this group that silently nods while the rest of the ideas crack jokes about horns and pitchforks.

THE OLD MAN looks at YOUTHFUL CYNICISM and waits. "Yes," he says. An awkward pause usually ensues at this point as the ideas in my head try to remember the question and then realize what THE OLD MAN's answer means. The silence grows until THE OLD MAN opens the big book in his arms again and begins to speak. "Yes. Except I've never read anything in this book about what he looks like. I have read that Jesus called him 'the father of lies.' Jesus said—"

YOUTHFUL CYNICISM interrupts again. "Let me guess: you're getting this quote from that big book in your arms?"

"Absolutely. According to the Keepers of the Sentence, according to those whose purpose in life was to transmit to others what Jesus had said, according to *them,* Jesus one time said that Satan 'was a murderer from the beginning, not holding to the truth, for there is no truth in him. When he lies, he speaks his native language, for he is a liar and the father of lies.'"[6]

YOUTHFUL CYNICISM nods condescendingly. "So Jesus called him a liar. That's cute."

THE DIRTY BEGGAR (who is a very dark idea living in my head[7]) doesn't look up but whispers a hoarse, barely audible "There's nothing cute about it." But few of the ideas in my head hear him.

YOUTHFUL CYNICISM does, though, and looks a bit scared. THE DIRTY BEGGAR is a shadowy idea, keeping to himself mostly. But when he does say something, it becomes clear that not many other ideas want to mess with him.

THE OLD MAN looks over at YOUTHFUL CYNICISM. "Jesus said that Satan only knows how to speak lies. And if the person of Jesus (and the ensuing church's message about that Jesus) was God's greatest moment of clarity, and his greatest effort at loving the little people he had created, then don't you think it stands to reason that Satan, God's adversary—"

"Would try to screw up that message?"

THE OLD MAN nods at the young idea in front of him. "Exactly."

"Wait!" At this point another idea pipes up. This new idea, BEWARE OF HYPERBOLE AND EXAGGERATION FROM IDEOLOGUES, continues in an accusing tone, "You're saying these other books were written by people who were *Satanists?*"

THE OLD MAN shakes his head. "Not at all. I'm saying it does not surprise me that books about Jesus that got the story all wrong were written. For both of the reasons I've given."

POWER ALWAYS CORRUPTS speaks up from her couch. "But someone had to make the call about which got in and which didn't. And how can you sit here today so willingly trusting that group of people?"

"Because it was the church"—THE OLD MAN

turns to face POWER ALWAYS CORRUPTS—"a church that was consumed with one purpose, only one reason for being: hearing the story of Jesus right and telling it right. That was their purpose and their calling! They were the Keepers of the Sentence, after all. And Jesus had sent his Wind to be around them and in them to help them live out this calling."

POWER ALWAYS CORRUPTS nods sadly. "And spread the true story of Jesus around the world, into every last country and culture."

"Yes." THE OLD MAN doesn't seem to notice her sadness.

At this point YOUTHFUL CYNICISM, looking at THE OLD MAN through his wispy bangs, starts up again. "But doesn't it seem a bit . . . *random* that God would use a book, of all things. And that you would have it right there in your hands?"

"Not random at all. Jesus himself (God in a little body, remember) acknowledged the Hebrew Scriptures. Those are the books that form the first part of this book in my arms. He quoted from them often, defended their divine status—that they had come from God—and even spoke strongly against the idea of trying to change those Hebrew Scriptures."

"You're talking about the Old Testament, right?"

"Exactly. These were books that recorded God's

communications for his people during Scene One. And this book had also come about through human processes, being passed on orally first, eventually getting written down by humans—a human process watched over by God. It didn't seem weird or random to Jesus that God had deemed it important and necessary to have a book or that God was capable of watching over the human process of creating that book."

YOUTHFUL CYNICISM keeps looking at THE OLD MAN. "Just like with the New Testament?"

THE OLD MAN stares back at the young, slouching idea. "Yeah."

One of the members of the Higher Criticism Gang yells from his spot against a far wall, "But there are plenty of contradictions between the two halves of that book you're holding. I know you are naive and uneducated, but you have to at least admit that Jesus changed a lot when he came on the scene and started teaching."

THE OLD MAN shakes his head. "Not at all, sir. Jesus was quite particular about that. Mind if I quote him?"

YOUTHFUL CYNICISM folds his arms and sits back in his couch. "And you're getting this two-thousand-year-old, very accurate quote from . . . ?"

THE OLD MAN smiles at this point. His fingers, veins showing through the pale skin, slowly turn several of the large, yellowed pages, and he starts to read, "Do not think that I have come to abolish the Law or the Prophets; I have not come to abolish them but to fulfill them."[8]

YOUTHFUL CYNICISM brushes his bangs aside. "I'm sorry. 'The Law and Prophets'?"

"That's what they called the Hebrew Bible, this 'Old' Testament."

"So why call it the 'Old' Testament if Jesus said he wasn't abolishing it?"

THE OLD MAN just looks at YOUTHFUL CYNICISM. "Because it's . . . *old*."

The young idea grins slightly. "Ah. And the 'New' Testament . . ."

"Is new."

"Gotcha. So Jesus dug the Hebrew Bible."

THE OLD MAN smiles again. "Yes. And defended it." THE OLD MAN takes his time slowly turning the pages, his old hands making a soft sound, almost like muted leaves, as he turns ancient page after ancient page. Finally he finds his place and reads, "Truly I tell you, until heaven and earth disappear, not the smallest letter, not the least stroke of a pen, will by any means disappear from the Law until everything is accomplished. Anyone who sets aside one of the least of these commands and teaches others accordingly will be called least in the kingdom of heaven."[9]

POWER ALWAYS CORRUPTS sits up a bit. "Sounds a little harsh, don't you think?"

THE OLD MAN shrugs. "It sounds, I think, like God must take these books of his words quite seriously, yes."

At this point some of the new ideas eye the big black book suspiciously. Others roll their eyes and make their way to an exit.

But THE CHURCH IS BANKRUPT (AND HAS HURT ME) has had enough. Debating stuff that happened two thousand years ago is one thing; she's more interested in what's been happening more recently. Each time he read from that black book on his lap, she sat there with that furrowed brow of hers and stewed more and more. At this point she finally loses it.

And that's when things get really interesting up in my head.

Chapter 5

CLUTCHING THE BIBLE TODAY

THE CHURCH IS BANKRUPT (AND HAS HURT ME) is most recognizable because of her furrowed brow. It always seems to be furrowed and there's a sort of wounded posture in her middle-aged manner. But not wounded as in weak and vulnerable. There's a definite strength in her, a solid strength. And always that furrowed brow.

She shakes her head, a touch of anger in her eyes, her brow aimed at THE OLD MAN. "But your church hasn't been doing a very good job of all that, have they, old man? The church teaches all kinds of different things! And there are so many different churches. And aren't they all clutching that same book you are? And aren't they disagreeing with each other left and right? To be honest, what I hear from the church doesn't sound so much like a clear Sentence as a babble, a cacophony, a centuries-old distracted concert!"

The middle-aged idea's voice echoes throughout

the living room of my mind. She looks around her, then looks back at THE OLD MAN, speaking more softly. "And the message we're getting from all that sure isn't that God loves us."

At this point THE OLD MAN nods his head slowly and closes his eyes. He pauses a long moment before speaking softly, "You're right."

"I'm right?" THE CHURCH IS BANKRUPT looks surprised. "Of course I'm right! God's idea for Scene Three isn't going so well, is it? Not according to plan at all. Which makes me doubt that cute little story of yours even more."

THE OLD MAN nods slowly, his grip not budging from the big book in his hands.

YOUTHFUL CYNICISM notices THE OLD MAN's hands. "So, how can you still clutch that book like you do?"

THE OLD MAN looks up at YOUTHFUL CYNICISM and then over to THE CHURCH IS BANKRUPT before speaking. "What you describe—the fighting in the church, the many disagreements, the divergent messages coming from the church—makes me want to clutch this book even tighter."

YOUTHFUL CYNICISM and THE CHURCH IS BANKRUPT look at each other with looks of confusion. YOUTHFUL CYNICISM looks back at THE OLD MAN. "Tighter?"

"Yes." THE OLD MAN's voice, though old, sounds calm and sure.

THE CHURCH IS BANKRUPT stares at THE OLD MAN. "Why cling to that book when clinging to it has obviously failed the church?"

THE OLD MAN's eyes meet hers. "Clinging to this book is not what is responsible for the fractures you describe."

YOUTHFUL CYNICISM chuckles to himself as if he's heard a good joke. "And I suppose you know exactly what's causing these fractures, old man?"

"Yes."

"Mind sharing your deep wisdom and insight with the rest of us?"

THE OLD MAN nods. "Of course." THE OLD MAN slowly opens the large book and begins searching for a page.

"You are so weird." YOUTHFUL CYNICISM smiles and shakes his head. "You think the answer to everything is in that book, don't you?"

THE OLD MAN smiles back. "Why do you think I clutch it so? Now, I believe I may have already read this to you before. 'Jesus Christ is the same yesterday and today and forever. Do not be carried away by all kinds of strange teachings.' "[1]

"Your point being?"

"The point *of this text* being that Jesus, the Sentence, does not change. Ever. But that men and women are going to be tempted to get carried away into strange teachings. And thus all these fractures in the church." THE OLD MAN looks back toward

THE CHURCH IS BANKRUPT as he continues, "Which makes me want to 'pay the most careful attention, therefore, to what we have heard, so that we do not drift away.' "[2]

An idea from the Enlightenment Gang stands up near the back wall of the living room in my head. He's wearing a one-piece outfit that looks like it came from the set of the original *Star Trek* show. His name is HUMANISM, and as everyone spins to see him, he speaks to THE OLD MAN in an impressive, anchorman-worthy voice. "You're just a quoting machine, aren't you? Have you ever had an original thought, old man?"

"All the time." THE OLD MAN smiles and nods as if remembering something funny. "And I test every single one of these *great original thoughts* of mine against this book."

HUMANISM, still standing, looks offended. "But that's so limiting. It's unnatural!"

THE OLD MAN keeps smiling and even chuckles. "To me, it's quite freeing."

"Freeing?" HUMANISM has his strong hands on his sculpted hips. "How can chaining your mind to that book be freeing?"

"Chaining my mind?!" THE OLD MAN's smile is gone and is replaced by a fire in his eyes. "This book *cuts* the chains that keep my mind strapped to this world. Without this book, I am stranded from God's thoughts and limited to petty human reasoning. Human thinking is mysterious and majestic in many ways, but it's a broken machine. My thinking can only walk along with a limp; my ideas are tiny things that have no wings but just flop around on this little earth. This book frees me from the dazzling deceptions that chain other people, that bind them and keep their minds from soaring on the heights of truth and reality and divine Wind."

HUMANISM, standing tall in his *Star Trek* outfit, looks offended. "Whoa. You're starting to freak me out! Do you really think all human reasoning is . . . *petty?*"

THE OLD MAN has flipped to a new page in the big black book before HUMANISM has even finished his question. His voice solemn, almost somber, he reads, "What things they do understand by instinct, like unreasoning animals—these are the very things that destroy them."[3]

THE DIRTY BEGGAR stirs in a far corner and mumbles under his breath—something about "forked tongues," I think. His voice sounds sad or angry and he's looking down at the floor in front of him, his head nodding slightly. But few ideas seem to notice him, and POWER ALWAYS CORRUPTS, slouching back in her couch, speaks with volume, "Well, you have a cute verse for everything, don't you?"

THE OLD MAN looks at POWER ALWAYS CORRUPTS and then looks back toward HUMANISM, who still stands proud and unashamed in his skin-tight outfit. "Not quite. Listen, I am not trying to debate you with 'cute' little verses." THE OLD MAN closes his eyes for a moment before proceeding more slowly. "I am trying to show you the testimony of the church. Every single author who wrote about the Sentence felt strongly that he was writing to preserve ultimate truth as found in Jesus, hearing the Sentence and repeating it to others. And every single one of them contrasted that task with the temptation to get sabotaged by mere human ideas. They knew these little, imperfect human sentences would woo people away from *the* Sentence, which was from God."

"Imperfect human sentences?" HUMANISM's well-trained voice echoes strongly throughout the living room in my head.

THE OLD MAN looks down at the big black book in his lap and closes his eyes. "I'm quoting from Paul here: 'See to it that no one takes you captive through hollow and deceptive philosophy, which depends on human tradition and the elemental spiritual forces of this world rather than on Christ.'"[4] THE OLD MAN opens his eyes and looks around. "Do you see it right there?"

HUMANISM looks unimpressed. "See what?"

"Paul is begging people to not be taken as slaves to mere human sentences. He's urging them to grab tightly onto *the* Sentence." THE OLD MAN looks from HUMANISM to THE CHURCH IS BANK-RUPT and then on to YOUTHFUL CYNICISM. "Paul writes that he strives to proclaim the true Sentence with all the energy he has because . . . Well, let me read here."

THE OLD MAN's fingers work the ancient pages with patience. When he finds the page he's looking for, he leans his old face closer and reads, "I want you to know how hard I am contending for you and for those at Laodicea, and for all who have not met me personally. My goal is that they may be encouraged in heart and united in love, so that they may have the full riches of complete understanding, in order that they may know the mystery of God, namely, Christ, in whom are hidden all the treasures of wisdom and knowledge."[5]

THE OLD MAN pauses and looks around him with wide eyes. "And do you know why Paul wrote all that to them?"

YOUTHFUL CYNICISM speaks up first. "We have no idea. Do tell."

THE OLD MAN continues reading. "I tell you this so that no one may deceive you by fine-sounding arguments."[6] He looks up from the page, smiling. "You see? Paul didn't want them to be trapped by so-called wisdom that comes from men but freed by the wisdom that came down from God. In other words, revelation trumps common sense every time!"

THE CHURCH IS BANKRUPT (AND HAS HURT ME) unfolds her arms and leans forward. "Then why all the fractured churches, why all the arguments, if this revelation is so great?"

THE OLD MAN looks in her eyes for a moment as if thinking. He shakes his head briefly and then leans forward slightly. "Will you take a three-part answer?"

General ruckus at this point. Several ideas get up and walk straight out of my head, muttering about "that ignorant old man and his three-part answers." Others laugh and joke with each other. HUMANISM finds his seat again, shaking his head and whispering to some of the Enlightenment Gang sitting near him.

THE CHURCH IS BANKRUPT (AND HAS HURT ME) looks around the room and, seeing it get relatively quiet, again nods to THE OLD MAN. "Why not?"

THE OLD MAN nods back. "OK. First, on the whole there's so much fracture and disagreement and varying messages because at times some within the church have loosened their grip on this book and have gotten carried away by all kinds of human ideas. They have been 'deceived by fine-sounding arguments,' as Paul put it."

THE CHURCH IS BANKRUPT looks down at THE OLD MAN's prized possession. "But they're still clutching that book, right?"

"Well, some of them. But some allow other books or ideas to strongly influence how they read this book. They allow human ideas to color their interpretation of this book."

PERSPECTIVE IS EVERYTHING, a woman wearing ornate jewelry that seems to have come from many different countries and cultures, very little of which matches, leans casually back in her rocking chair. She speaks calmly, smoothly. "But we all have a different perspective, right? How can you expect any two people to read it the same way?"

THE OLD MAN looks over at this decorated, jingling woman. I can tell at once that he knows her and doesn't like her. "I expect that because it is the Sentence—it is really a quite clear historical story that is found here in this book. And I expect that because God sent his Wind to remind us of everything he said, to make sure we hear the Sentence correctly."

PERSPECTIVE IS EVERYTHING laughs a calm laugh as she continues rocking slowly in her chair, her multinational jewelry continuing to jingle exotically. "But that's impossible! Everyone has a different view, a different take. That's the nature of the world. You are incredibly naive if you assume that there can be some objective written Sentence that everyone should be able to read the same way."

THE OLD MAN stares at her. "Just as naive as Jesus himself, I guess."

PERSPECTIVE IS EVERYTHING slows her rocking and motions with her hands, causing the various bracelets around her wrists to sound. "What do you mean, old man?"

"Jesus time and time again confronted the religious leaders of the Jews and accused them of misinterpreting the Hebrew Bible. And his accusations show implicitly that he believed the words of God were clear and that these leaders were purposefully misinterpreting them and that this gross misinterpretation was not surprising."

THE OLD MAN flips more pages at this point, his hands a bit shaky. When his patient hands find the right page, he speaks. "Listen to some of his accusations. 'Isaiah was right when he prophesied about you hypocrites; as it is written: "These people honor me with their lips, but their hearts are far from me. They worship me in vain; their teachings are merely human rules." You have let go of the commands of God and are holding on to human traditions.' "[7]

YOUTHFUL CYNICISM shakes his head, and his bangs go wild. "So Jesus did it too!"

THE OLD MAN looks confused. "Did what?"

YOUTHFUL CYNICISM smiles. "Cheated! He quoted from the Hebrew Bible to defend the Hebrew Bible."

THE OLD MAN nods. "Sure. The Law and the Prophets made it clear what the commands of God were *and* that there would be people who would let go of those commands."

THE CHURCH IS BANKRUPT (AND HAS HURT ME) leans forward, looking semi-interested. "And these religious leaders had just let go of the Hebrew Bible?"

THE OLD MAN looks over at her and shakes his head. "Not at all. That's the whole point. They clung to it but then let their own ideas, or the ideas of other humans, color their reading of it. When they defended themselves against this last accusation, Jesus made his point very clearly. He said, 'You have a fine way of setting aside the commands of God in order to observe your own traditions!'[8] Then he read from the Hebrew Bible and showed them how drastically they were deceiving people about it. He ended by proclaiming, 'Thus you nullify the word of God by your tradition that you have handed down. And you do many things like that.'[9] He had really sharp words for them."

THE CHURCH IS BANKRUPT nods, her brow furrowed even more. "So they were some really bad guys?"

THE OLD MAN looks at her and shrugs. "I don't know if that's the point. The point is they were handing down *'their own traditions'* and Jesus confronted them about that. So if Jesus was naive in assuming that it was possible to receive the words of God and that it was also possible to let go of those words by allowing one's own ideas to sway the reading, then I suppose I am naive in exactly the same way."

THE CHURCH IS BANKRUPT leans forward. "So, what are you saying?"

"I'm answering your question. Why are there so many different sentences coming from the church? On the whole, it's because we are tempted to read the Sentence through the lens of our own sentences. Which makes me want to clutch this Bible more and more and submit every thought I have, every new book I read, every little bit of common sense, to this big black book."

PERSPECTIVE IS EVERYTHING motions with her hand, causing a jingle of jewelry to enter the living room in my head. "Still sounds simplistic to me."

THE OLD MAN nods. "But that was just my first point."

PERSPECTIVE IS EVERYTHING smiles and continues rocking calmly. "Ah yes. Your incredible three-part answer." She pauses, most of the ideas in my head staring at her and her exotic outfit and jewelry. She relishes the attention and then looks up at THE OLD MAN. "Your second reason for the state of the church's message?"

"We have an enemy."

YOUTHFUL CYNICISM chuckles to himself. "Satan again?"

TRAGEDY points his old, tired eyes at YOUTHFUL CYNICISM from across the room with a look that makes me think he'd walk right over and show this young fellow a thing or two if he weren't so tired. THE OLD MAN, though, smiles at YOUTHFUL CYNICISM. "Yes. The book I am holding tells me he is real, he is panicked and his primary weapon is deception."

THE CHURCH IS BANKRUPT looks interested and nods slightly. "So, you're saying he is having his way with the church's message?"

"I'm sure he's busy blurring whatever lines he can, whispering whatever kinds of deceptions he can. And some people listen."

HUMANISM stays seated but allows his impressive voice to float up and fill the living room in my head. "You really are old-fashioned. You realize that, don't you? We're here in the twenty-first century, you know. And you're talking about Satan."

THE OLD MAN looks back toward HUMANISM. "I know. That's my third point."

"Your third point?" HUMANISM looks around at the ideas sitting near him and they shrug.

"Yes." THE OLD MAN looks around from idea to idea, his eyes blinking, perhaps with fatigue. He goes on, his voice shaky but resolute as usual. "On the whole, I think the church's message can seem fractured because of the human tendency to think new thoughts rather than just stick with the old Sentence. And, on the whole, I think our enemy loves encouraging that tendency. But a small bit of

the disagreements come from the church strug-
gling to respond to this changing world. This
twenty-first-century world. That's my third point."

THE CHURCH IS BANKRUPT stares at the frail
old man. "What? The church doesn't know how to
respond to this age we're in?"

THE OLD MAN nods slightly. "Well, at times leaders of the church have to respond to new cultural or
social realities. And they don't always respond in
the same ways."

"Like what?"

"Well, for example, in my book there are stories
of the early church having to grapple with non-Jews
hearing the Sentence and loving it. The first student-followers were all Jews. But then all of a sud-
den they had to figure out if non-Jews who heard
the story should grow their sideburns out and stop
eating bacon. And it took the church a while to figure it all out."

YOUTHFUL CYNICISM speaks softly, more softly
than he usually does. "So your third point is that
the church is living a complicated life like the rest
of us?"

THE OLD MAN looks over at YOUTHFUL CYNI-
CISM THAT QUESTIONS ALL AUTHORITY. "Not exactly. Some of the mixed messages you hear are
these kinds of internal dialogues. But on the
whole—remember this is a three-part answer; you
can handle nuance, can't you?—*on the whole,* I think

it's the human tendency to get distracted by clever new ideas and our enemy's encouragement of that which are to blame for what you see."

"OK, fine." YOUTHFUL CYNICISM's voice is a little louder. "But it still doesn't seem to me like Scene Three of your cute story is working out very well. Which makes it a really hard story to believe."

"Oh, Scene Three is wonderful." THE OLD MAN smiles and gets a faraway look in his eyes.

YOUTHFUL CYNICISM brushes his bangs to the side. "What?! But you just said—"

"Listen, son. What do you think is going to get more time on the evening news and more column space in the newspapers—the beautiful chorus of the church proclaiming and celebrating the Sentence globally, or cat-fighting debates that are full of sparks and name-calling?"

THE OLD MAN's back gets a little less bent over as he continues. "Do you think it's the deep, humanly inexplicable unity among Christians of every nation and tribe and race and social class that will get the press or the few bitter, line-drawing, hate-filled rants of those who are more centered on some new topic than on Jesus?"

THE OLD MAN stops even though it appears he has more to say. As he's catching his breath, BEWARE OF HYPERBOLE AND EXAGGERATION FROM IDEOLOGUES butts in. "What are you saying? The media are deceiving me?"

THE OLD MAN catches his breath and continues a bit more slowly, more softly. "The media are shrewdly providing a product to a voyeuristic society. And the media are ignoring the miraculous, joyful story of the spread of the Sentence, because we live in a world that has rejected that Sentence. So don't judge Scene Three just by reading *Newsweek*. There's nothing surprising about a world that rejects the Sentence or about leaders who are tempted to stray into strange ideas. This book I'm holding makes it perfectly clear that would be part of Scene Three. Which makes me clutch this book even more tightly."

YOUTHFUL CYNICISM smiles at THE OLD MAN. "You and your big black book, huh? A quote a minute." YOUTHFUL CYNICISM is genuinely smiling. Almost looks like he's warming up to the old guy.

But don't worry. He *is* YOUTHFUL CYNICISM, after all. And he *is* surrounded by plenty of other ideas that look ready to strangle THE OLD MAN if he starts reading one more stiff old quote from that dusty book of his. Which means we're not necessarily in for a calm, hand-holding kind of ending.

Not all the ideas up in my head get along, you see. And my head does want order. And so sometimes I have a sense that something's gotta give.

Chapter 6

THE MYTH OF
PROVING IT

Sometimes the conversation in the living room in my head goes on for quite a while when THE OLD MAN's been telling his story. In other words, lots of stuff to think about. Too much to tell about it all in detail here.

Sometimes JADED AND PISSED (a younger cousin of YOUTHFUL CYNICISM who can be quite sarcastic) asks why the big black book is black and why there are gold-edged pages. "Why do you have to have those little ribbons in the book and carry it around in a little satchel?" he asks, his voice making it clear that he's not really looking for an answer.

At other times the Higher Criticism Gang comes back into my head and peppers THE OLD MAN with more technical questions. "Which ancient manuscripts are being used to come up with the English translations we're using today? And why are there so many different translations in English?" But because they were not there to hear THE OLD MAN's story or his answers to previous questions, most of what THE OLD MAN says doesn't make much sense to them.

Some ideas have specific content questions. For example, WE'RE ALL OK asks about heaven and hell and whether one can really believe all of that. But when THE OLD MAN starts reading to WE'RE ALL OK, the younger idea quickly loses interest and doesn't listen to what THE OLD MAN reads. It's like that with many of the ideas that ask detailed questions about verses from the Bible they see as confusing or contradictory or offensive. They rarely sit still and listen while THE OLD MAN reads from that black book.

Some ideas ask THE OLD MAN about the ending of the story, and he smiles and starts to tell them about Scene Four, the story of Jesus coming back to the world one last time. There's plenty of laughter and derisive hoots during that part of the conversation. Through all the noise, barely any of the ideas actually hear THE OLD MAN's answers.

But toward the end, when YOUTHFUL CYNICISM grows bored with the various debates and questions and three-part answers, he leans far forward and speaks forcefully to THE OLD MAN. "But you can't prove it, can you? There's something circular about all this. What you read in that book makes you want to hold onto it. But you can't prove that it is the Word of God, can you? You can't prove that everything in it is true, can you? You can't even assure me that the writers really were trying to be faithful to what really happened, can you?"

THE OLD MAN responds calmly. "Not at all."

"What?" YOUTHFUL CYNICISM looks a bit surprised and shrugs. "And that doesn't make you doubt your firm grip?"

THE OLD MAN looks at YOUTHFUL CYNICISM and smiles. "Let me ask you a question."

YOUTHFUL CYNICISM shrugs. "OK."

"Can you prove to me that the writers of the New Testament purposely invented a false story about Jesus so they could start a new religion?"

"Can I prove it?"

"Can you prove it?"

YOUTHFUL CYNICISM looks over at POWER ALWAYS CORRUPTS and the other ideas sitting near him before looking back at THE OLD MAN. "What do you want? For me to tell you my reasoning again? To hear it from a bunch of experts on religion and history? I'm not sure anything will prove it to you, you're so stubborn."

THE OLD MAN looks back calmly. "Is it really my stubbornness, son? Or is it more true to say that *proving* something is a questionable affair. In the end *you* believe the people who tell you a story about the Bible and its writing. And *I* believe other people who tell me a story about the Bible and its writing. We both trust a story. In the end, we are both believing in a story."

YOUTHFUL CYNICISM shrugs. "Are you insinuating that nothing can be proven?"

"Well, using scientific language to talk about history—for that is what we're talking about here— is a little tenuous." THE OLD MAN looks thoughtfully at YOUTHFUL CYNICISM as if collecting his thoughts. "For example, tell me: what country was the first to land men on the moon?"

YOUTHFUL CYNICISM's eyes grow wide with confusion. "You mean America? The U.S.?"

THE OLD MAN smiles at YOUTHFUL CYNICISM. "Oh, *America* was the first country to land men on the moon?"

"Yeah. What's your point?"

"Can you *prove* it to me?"

"That America was the first country?"

THE OLD MAN nods. "Yeah. Prove it."

YOUTHFUL CYNICISM shrugs and shakes his head, looking again at the ideas sitting near him. "What do you want? Video footage, newspaper clippings, official NASA logs, the testimony of any person on the street that you would ask? What are you getting at?"

THE OLD MAN's gaze is steady. "How do you know the astronauts really landed on the moon? Or that we were the first? Were you up there? What if those newspaper articles and video footage are de-

ceiving you? You never saw it happen with your
own eyes, did you?"

"No, but . . ."

"So you are choosing to trust what you read and
what other people are telling you. You believe their
story. You never saw it for yourself, did you? In fact,
you don't even know if the moon really exists,
do you?" THE OLD MAN winks at YOUTHFUL
CYNICISM.

"OK, I get your point."

THE OLD MAN's face turns serious again. "Listen, we are all choosing to believe something. We
can't really *prove* much to a skeptic, can we? We are
all believing. In someone, some people, some feeling of common sense, some story or . . . *something*."

YOUTHFUL CYNICISM pauses for a moment,
looking at THE OLD MAN in front of him.

POWER ALWAYS CORRUPTS jumps in. "But believing that Americans were the first on the moon
without being able to prove it is one thing. Why do
you believe the testimony of this book despite the
fact that you can't prove it?"

THE OLD MAN slowly touches the black book
that takes up his whole lap. "For all the reasons
I've told you. Because of the story. Because each of
the authors of this New Testament give us the
same insight into his reason for writing. They had
received something incredible and had a new—
and joyful—mission in life: to preserve the mes-

sage they had heard and repeat it to others. That's why they were writing. And I find the message they passed on to be incredible and consistent and life changing. And I find myself gripped by the same passion that gripped the early church: to tell that story over and over, guarding against anyone or anything or any internal impulse that might cause me to drift from the message as I have received it."

THE OLD MAN is sitting up straight at this point, his arms tight around the book on his lap. His voice begins to rise in volume, though it still retains a scent of frailness. "The only hope for the church here in Scene Three is humble leaders who aren't above being receivers and witnesses. The hope for the church is the Wind of God that accompanies her on this task. The hope is receiving this message and sticking to it and constantly rubbing off everything else that would want to stick to it. That's why I cling to this book, why I encourage people to be Keepers of the Sentence."

"And it's just that simple, huh? You and your book there." YOUTHFUL CYNICISM looks down at the big black book.

"This is received truth. Revelation from God. His clearest Sentence ever. The church has received this message. And this pulsing, living message itself calls her to pass that message on to others. For it's only in that message that it's possible to hear so clearly from the invisible God. This book tells exactly what he's like, exactly how much he loves his people and what exactly they were put on this little world for in the first place." THE OLD MAN has a faraway look in his eyes again.

THE OLD MAN living in my head tends to get emotional like that at the end. Which most new ideas have a hard time with. He catches his breath. He looks around at the room of ideas living in my head, his voice nearly spent. "Do you see why I clutch it so?"

YOUTHFUL CYNICISM meets THE OLD MAN's eyes. "I think I understand what makes *you* clutch it like that. You seem quite convinced."

Sometimes, after he's done, the other ideas will start telling their own stories to THE OLD MAN. And he will ask them questions. And they will respond to him. And (this is kind of funny) they always seem to get emotional toward the end of their stories as well.

And, in the end, I let him stay.

Why? Why allow such an old geezer to stay up in my head? For the same reason I let any idea stay up there—because I like his story. Because I really like the answers he gives to the other ideas up in my head. Because I like the questions he asks these other, more popular ideas. Because my life is different and more healthy and interesting and . . . *sane* since he's moved in. All ideas have consequences, after all. And the consequences in my life from this old guy have been, in a word, wonderful.

In fact, so many parts of me like THE OLD MAN CLUTCHING THE BIG BLACK BIBLE that I've made an agreement with the old guy that I won't go kicking him out on a whim. In other words, this idea is a real conviction of mine. In fact, I've given THE OLD MAN Permanent Resident status in my head. He actually has special privileges and is higher up on the social hierarchy that exists up there among ideas.[1] Several ideas have been kicked out because they didn't get along with the old guy so well. He's got real seniority now, and other ideas get the drift that if they upset the guy, they may be sent packing. So, if they want to stay, they try to work it out with THE OLD MAN.

I'll be honest, he still makes me uncomfortable at times, and his old-fashioned outfit really is ridiculous looking in certain settings. I've even gone and kicked him out a couple of times in the past. Boy, did that shake things up! A Permanent Resident getting kicked out? The fireworks flew then! The whole social hierarchy of the house was thrown into chaos.

But, over time, I've always taken him back in. It's just that story of his and those answers he gives and . . . and the way his presence in my head changes the place. Anyway, he's been a Permanent Resident for years now.

And, old-fashioned though he may be, I'm glad I can say there's an old man living in my head. An old man clutching a big black Bible.

CONCLUSION: YOUR HEAD

If your head works anything like mine, then by your reading this book, THE OLD MAN has walked right into your head as well. Ideas are like that: like people who come into your head and interact with all the other ideas living there. So, um . . . THE OLD MAN's living in your head now too. Or at least visiting.

Maybe you're ready to kick him out right now. Maybe you hear the whistles and barked comments from some of the other ideas in your mind already. My advice is this: let 'em work it out.

Let them tell each other their stories. Pepper *them all* with questions. And see how things shake out.

That's what we've been given brains for, after all. To think. To let the ideas work it out as we bring them all into the living room of our minds and ask them to interact with each other.

But remember, it's your head. It's your house of

living ideas. No one in there gets to boss other ideas around—without your permission. No one gets to stay, no one has to leave, without your say-so.

So work it out. This is the job of humans—to philosophize, to think, to be in charge of our heads. THE OLD MAN has gone and walked right into the house of your head. He's in there now. It's up to you to figure out what to do with him.

It's your head, after all.

NOTES

introduction: my head

[1]To get a more comprehensive view of how things work up in my head, you'd have to read *All the Ideas Living in My Head: One Guy's Musings About Truth,* where I give a full tour of my upstairs and how thinking tends to go on up there. It's a tell-all about how ideas behave in my head, the different types of ideas there are, why certain ideas get special privileges, how my mind interacts with my heart and soul, how I talk with others about their ideas and what, exactly, I think about McDonald's French fries. Among other things.

chapter 3: the writers of the bible

[1]John 15:26-27

[2]Luke 24:48; Matthew 28:19-20

[3]Luke 1:1-4

[4]1 John 1:1, 3

[5]SOURCE CRITICISM has lots of questions for THE OLD MAN. Lots. And he has his own story to tell too. It's a great story and THE OLD MAN has plenty of questions when SOURCE CRITICISM is through telling it. These two go at it a lot. There's too much to go into it all right here, but I will say that as the two talk about the writing and compiling of the Bible, SOURCE CRITICISM tends to focus on *how* it was written and compiled,

while THE OLD MAN tends to focus on *why* it was written and compiled. Come to think of it, the two tend to disagree in places about *who* did that writing and compiling as well. If you're interested in more detail on their conversations, I'd recommend reading *The New Testament Documents: Are They Reliable?* by F. F. Bruce or *The Old Testament Documents: Are They Reliable & Relevant?* by Walter C. Kaiser Jr. Every time I look at those books, these two ideas start talking with each other.

[6] 1 Corinthians 2:2; 15:3

[7] 2 Timothy 1:14

[8] For example, sometimes he'll read, "The things you have heard me say . . . entrust to reliable people who will also be qualified to teach others" (2 Timothy 2:2).

[9] In case you're curious, he'll often read Titus 1:9: "He must hold firmly to the trustworthy message as it has been taught."

[10] Hebrews 2:1, 3

[11] He quotes from Peter ("We did not follow cleverly devised stories when we told you about the coming of our Lord Jesus Christ in power, but we were eyewitnesses of his majesty," 2 Peter 1:16) and even from Jude when he's really on a roll ("I felt compelled to write and urge you to contend for the faith that the Lord has once for all entrusted to us, his people," Jude 3).

[12] John 14:26

chapter 4: getting the story wrong

[1] For more on Sexy Ideas (and other types of ideas, such as Pointy Ideas and Back Door Ideas), see the original tour of my head, *All the Ideas Living in My Head: One Guy's Musings About Truth*.

²Colossians 2:8

³2 Peter 2:3

⁴The verses he tends to read about these so-called false teachers are from each of the New Testament authors. Among these verses are 1 John 4:5 ("They are from the world and therefore speak from the viewpoint of the world, and the world listens to them"), Hebrews 13:8-9 ("Jesus Christ is the same yesterday and today and forever. Do not be carried away by all kinds of strange teachings"), James 3:15 ("Such 'wisdom' does not come down from heaven but is earthly, unspiritual, demonic") and Jude 19 ("These are the people who divide you, who follow mere natural instincts and do not have the Spirit").

⁵For more on this canonization process, refer to F. F. Bruce's *The New Testament Documents: Are They Reliable?*

⁶John 8:44

⁷You can get to know this idea more intimately, if you want, though not many people enjoy the experience, exactly. I introduce him and allow him to speak for himself in *The Dirty Beggar Living in My Head: One Guy's Musings About Evil and Hell.*

⁸Matthew 5:17

⁹Mathew 5:18-19

chapter 5: clutching the Bible today

¹Hebrews 13:8-9

²Hebrews 2:1

³Jude 10

⁴Colossians 2:8

⁵Colossians 2:1-3

⁶Colossians 2:4

⁷Mark 7:6-8

[8]Mark 7:9
[9]Mark 7:13

chapter 6: the myth of proving it

[1]For more on this social hierarchy and Permanent Resident status up in my head, check out the initial tour of my head, *All the Ideas Living in My Head: One Guy's Musings About Truth*.

ONE GUY'S HEAD SERIES

A bunch of ideas are running around in Don Everts's head. Some are permanent residents. Others are visitors, just passing through. When they all get together, some odd things start happening.

All the Ideas Living in My Head: One Guy's Musings About Truth, ISBN: 978-0-8308-3611-6

The Old Man Living in My Head: One Guy's Musings About the Bible, ISBN: 978-0-8308-3612-3

The Dirty Beggar Living in My Head: One Guy's Musings About Evil & Hell, ISBN: 978-0-8308-3613-0

The Fingerless Lady Living in My Head: One Guy's Musings About Tolerance, ISBN: 978-0-8308-3614-7

LIKEWISE. *Go and do.*

A man comes across an ancient enemy, beaten and left for dead. He lifts the wounded man onto the back of a donkey and takes him to an inn to tend to the man's recovery. Jesus tells this story and instructs those who are listening to "go and do likewise."

Likewise books explore a compassionate, active faith lived out in real time. When we're skeptical about the status quo, Likewise books challenge us to create culture responsibly. When we're confused about who we are and what we're supposed to be doing, Likewise books help us listen for God's voice. When we're discouraged by the troubled world we've inherited, Likewise books encourage us to hold onto hope.

In this life we will face challenges that demand our response. Likewise books face those challenges with us so we can act on faith.

likewisebooks.com